Saving Animals with Science

Bionic Animals

Tracy Sue Walker

Lerner Publications ◆ Minneapolis

For Mom and Dad

Lerner Publications Company
An imprint of Lerner Publishing Group, Inc.
241 First Avenue North
Minneapolis, MN 55401 USA

For reading levels and more information, look up this title at www.lernerbooks.com.

Main body text set in Adrianna Regular.
Typeface provided by Chank.

Photo Editor: Nicole Berglund

Library of Congress Cataloging-in-Publication Data

Names: Walker, Tracy Sue, author.
Title: Bionic animals / Tracy Sue Walker.
Description: Minneapolis : Lerner Publications, 2024. | Series: Searchlight books. Saving animals with science | Includes bibliographical references and index. | Audience: Ages 8–11 | Audience: Grades 4–6 | Summary: "An elephant lost one of its front legs and had trouble getting around. Scientists got to work and through trial and error built the elephant a bionic limb. Discover how science is helping injured animals"—Provided by publisher.
Identifiers: LCCN 2023009283 (print) | LCCN 2023009284 (ebook) | ISBN 9798765609125 (lib. bdg.) | ISBN 9798765624777 (pbk.) | ISBN 9798765617182 (epub)
Subjects: LCSH: Veterinary surgery—Juvenile literature. | Prosthesis—Juvenile literature. | Bionics—Juvenile literature. | Medical technology—Juvenile literature. | BISAC: JUVENILE NONFICTION / Animals / Animal Welfare
Classification: LCC SF911 .W35 2024 (print) | LCC SF911 (ebook) | DDC 636.089/7—dc23/eng/20230512

LC record available at https://lccn.loc.gov/2023009283
LC ebook record available at https://lccn.loc.gov/2023009284

Manufactured in the United States of America
2-1011102-51590-4/18/2024

Table of Contents

Chapter 1

BIONIC WONDERS

At seven months old, an elephant named Mosha lost part of her front left leg. She had stepped on a land mine, a bomb that is buried in the ground and explodes when stepped on or driven over. Without part of her front leg, more pressure was put on her back and other legs. An elephant foundation found and rescued Mosha. Orthopedic surgeon Dr. Therdchai Jivacate designed a new leg for her. Orthotics is a branch of medicine that deals with designing and fitting medical support devices.

Jivacate created the leg using plastic, sawdust, and metal. Before getting her new leg, Mosha leaned against railings to take the pressure off her body. But after her prothesis, or replacement leg, was put on, she was able to walk without pressure on her back and legs.

Mosha has her prosthetic leg attached in 2016.

Bionics uses the science behind how things naturally work to solve engineering problems. For animals such as Mosha with limb differences, scientists study how their limbs work to create a prosthesis. Prosthetics can improve some animals' lives.

German shepherd Mitzi has a prosthetic back foot.

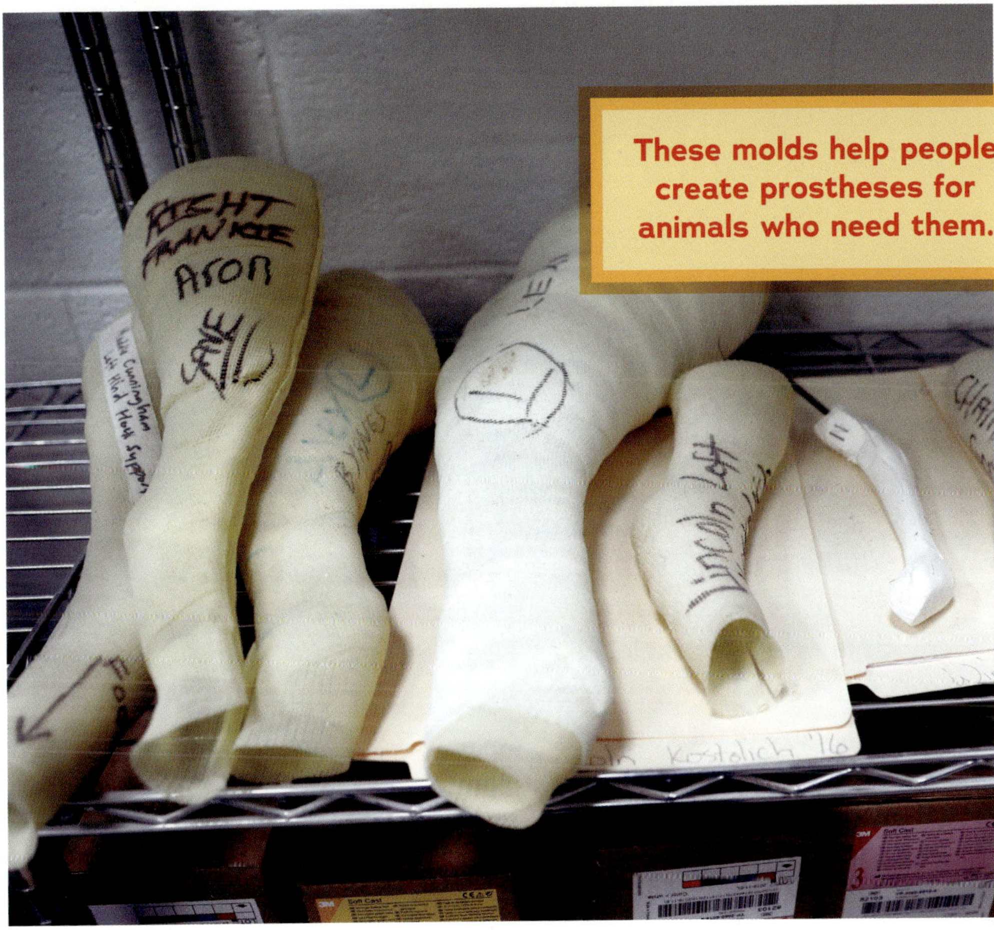

These molds help people create prostheses for animals who need them.

Building a Bionic Limb

Before creating a bionic limb, scientists study how limbs work to know how to re-create them. They also make a cast of the animal's body where the prosthesis will attach. Then they use computer software and 3D printers to make models of these limbs. Next, scientists test their models to see which one works best. They might redesign their models or design new ones.

Deep Dive

3D Printers and Prosthetics

To create an object, 3D printers layer material. They often use plastic, but they can also make things with metal, graphite, and carbon fiber.

These printers have been groundbreaking for prosthetics. First computer software creates 3D models. This lets scientists see how prosthetics will work in the real world. Once they find the best model, they print the limb.

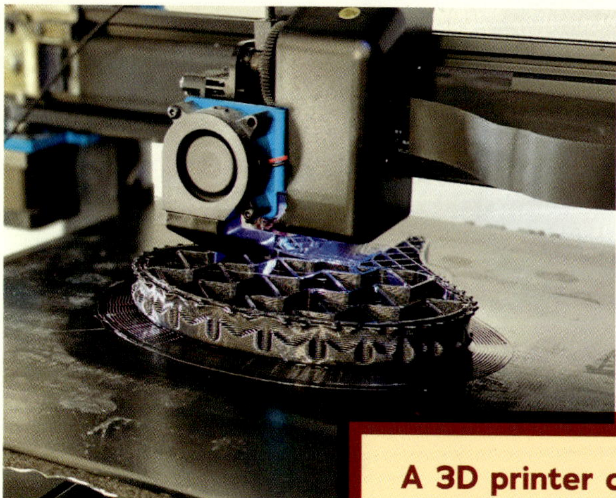

A 3D printer creating a bionic foot for a dog

Monika runs around with her prostheses.

Once they find the best design, they build the limb and attach it to the animal. As new technology develops, scientists will have more ways to help animals.

Chapter 2

LAND BIONICS

Bionics has helped Mosha the elephant survive. Discover how this technology assisted other animals that mainly live on the land.

Vito's New Legs

A cat named Vito was hit by a car and lost his two back legs in 2018. Vito's vets made him temporary back legs with sturdy sticks and cotton balls. But he needed something more permanent to get around.

Since cats jump a lot, Vito's vets decided to add springs to his new legs. Eventually, they finished making his permanent legs with metal and other materials. Vito is back on the prowl and has even gone on to become an internet star.

VITO WAS THE FIRST CAT IN ITALY TO RECEIVE PROSTHESES.

Boonie, a three-year-old goat that got his leg caught in barbed wire

Bionic Boonie

In 2008, a goat called Boonie was tied outside. His hoof got tangled in a rope. He ended up losing one of his front hooves. Boonie's vet was afraid he would get arthritis in his remaining hoof. Arthritis is joint pain or joint disease.

Boonie's owner, Marna Peterson, discovered OrthoPets. The company creates prostheses for animals. OrthoPets sent Peterson a temporary prosthetic leg. The top had foam lining, which made an imprint of his leg. OrthoPets used that imprint to make a permanent prosthesis that would fit him. When Boonie first got his new leg, he hopped on it, but later he learned to walk on it. It also prevented him from getting arthritis in his remaining front hoof.

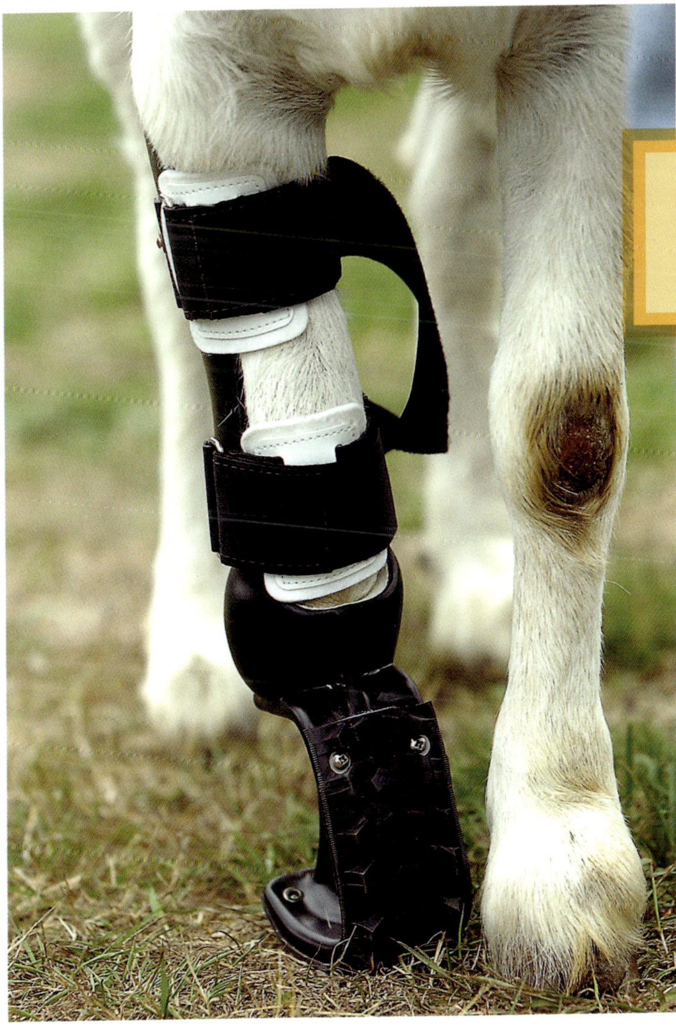

Boonie's new hoof has a plastic and rubber base.

Most giraffes are able to stand and walk thirty minutes after being born.

Helping Msituni Walk

A giraffe named Msituni was born at the San Diego Zoo in 2022. Most giraffe calves are able to stand and walk. But Msituni had trouble bending her front legs. After making 3D images of her legs, Msituni's vet created braces to help Msituni's front legs bend. They also made hoof extenders for her back legs since the joints in those legs were weak. The zoo reached out to an orthotic clinic.

The zoo and clinic made molds of Msituni's legs and then made braces. They made sure the braces let her stand and lie down. After thirty-nine days of wearing braces, Msituni's legs healed.

Spotlight On

Derrick Campana

Derrick Campana is the founder of Bionic Pets, a company that makes prostheses for animals. He has helped over twenty-five thousand animals. Before helping animals, Campana made mobility devices for humans. In 2005, he made a prosthesis for a dog. After seeing how few options there were for animals needing prostheses, he decided to focus on helping animals. In his TV show, *The Wizard of Paws*, viewers see how he makes these devices.

Derrick Campana shakes the bionic paw of a golden retriever.

Chapter 3

AIR BIONICS

New technology is supporting flying animals. Discover how bionics helps birds.

Building Beaks

Beauty the bald eagle was hit with a bullet to her beak. She lost her upper beak. Beauty couldn't eat or drink. Wildlife specialist and biologist Jane Veltkamp rescued Beauty. Her organization, Birds of Prey Northwest, helps sick and injured birds.

Beauty's prosthetic attaches to her beak.

Some birds can regrow their beaks, but it takes a long time. Beauty needed a new beak so she could eat and drink until hers regrew. Veltkamp worked with a team that included her dentist to make a beak for Beauty. They made the beak with a 3D printer and attached it to Beauty. She was able to eat and drink again!

Grecia after losing part of her beak in an attack

Grecia, a toucan, was attacked by people and lost her upper beak. Toucans need their beaks to eat, drink, and keep themselves cool. Unlike bald eagles, toucans can't completely regrow their beaks.

Rescate Wildlife Rescue Center took Grecia in. The animal rehabilitation center worked with a 3D printing company to make Grecia a prosthetic beak. They looked at different toucans' beaks to figure out how to make one for Grecia. Then they made a two-piece beak out of nylon. The first part was glued to Grecia's upper beak. The second part attaches to the first part with a pin. That way Grecia's caretakers can take off the second part for cleaning.

Grecia's new beak was created by a 3D printer.

Mia stands on her prosthetic foot.

Mechanical Mia

Mia, a bearded vulture, was missing a foot. When she was a baby, Mia's parents used wool to build their nest. The wool tangled around Mia's ankle and damaged her foot. Her foot had to be amputated, or removed. But Mia needed her leg to hunt and walk.

Scientists at a medical school decided to help. Since vultures are large, the leg would have to support her weight. They designed a bionic leg that connected to her leg bone. After they attached the leg, Mia could hunt and walk again.

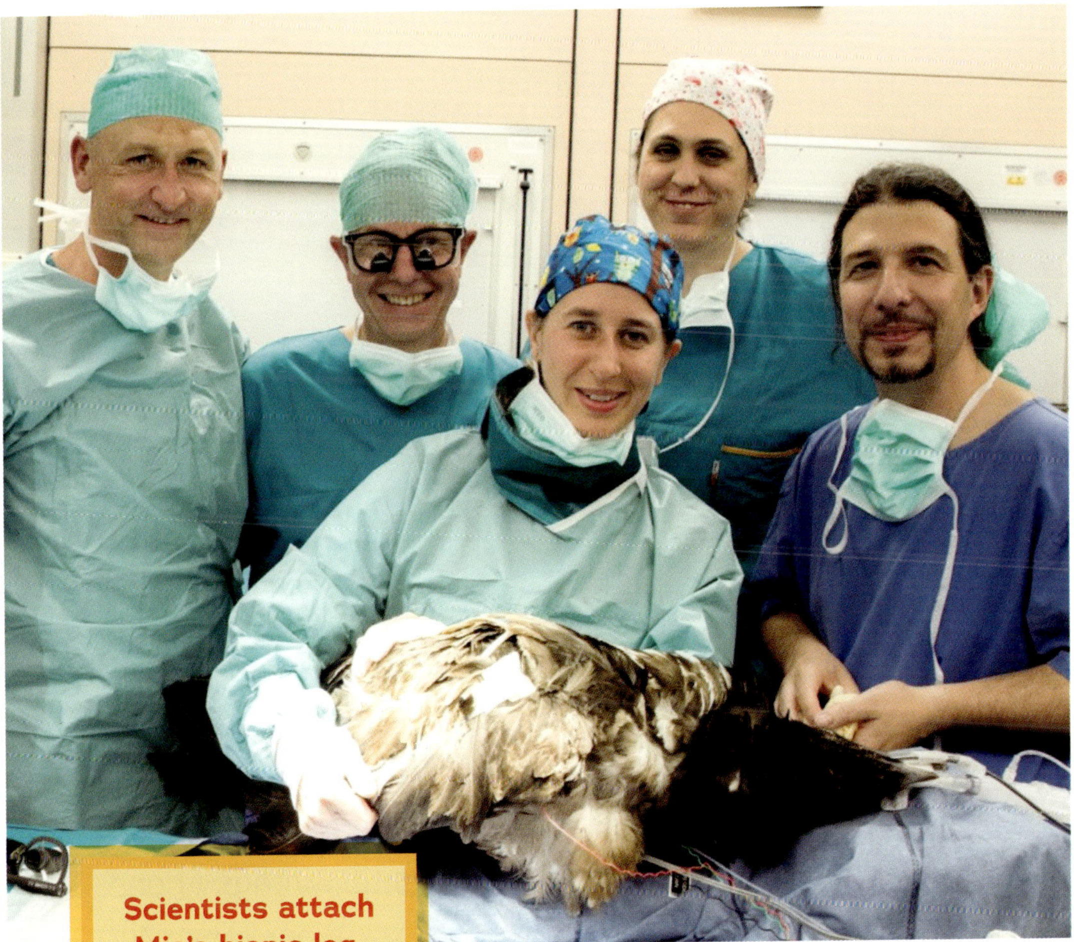

Scientists attach Mia's bionic leg.

Chapter 4

WATER BIONICS

From fins to tails, discover how bionics is helping water animals.

Swimming with Ease

Sea turtle Allison was attacked by a predator and lost three of her flippers. People found her on a beach and took her to an animal rehabilitation center. With only one flipper, Allison would swim in circles around her tank. Researchers began working on a prosthesis. They tried

one model with a back flipper, but it didn't work. So they made more models including a wet suit that fit over her shell with a dorsal fin on the back. Finally, they created a prosthesis that clips onto her shell with a fin on her back. The fin acts similar to a rudder, an underwater blade on a boat that helps it change direction. That made swimming easier for Allison.

Predators aren't the only threat to sea turtles and their flippers. Boats and fishing nets can damage their flippers too, and without their fins, sea turtles can't move well.

Spotlight On
AUT BioDesign Lab

When a female sea turtle loses a limb, it's harder for her to come onto shore and lay eggs. That could mean fewer sea turtles in the future. AUT BioDesign Lab in New Zealand is helping to solve this problem.

Researchers from AUT BioDesign Lab wanted to create a prosthetic flipper that moves like a real flipper. They made several flippers and built a robotic turtle to test their design. The robotic turtle moved like a real turtle. Engineers saw how their flipper moved and worked to make it better. Researchers built the best design. They are using these flippers to help injured sea turtles.

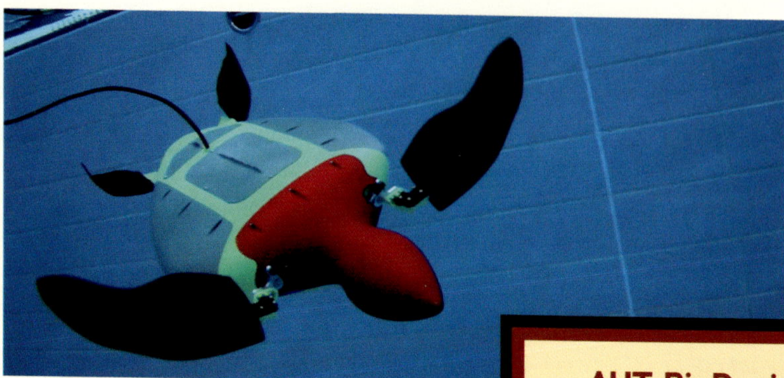

AUT BioDesign Lab's flipper model

Winter's new tail helps her propel herself forward and change direction.

A Dolphin Tale

In 2005, a dolphin named Winter became tangled in a crab trap and lost part of her tail. She was rescued and taken to Florida's Clearwater Marine Aquarium. It took a prosthetic clinic a year and a half to create a new tail for Winter. The tail needed to move with her full spine and stay on when she leaped in the air. The clinic also developed a gel liner to help Winter's tail stick to her body. Winter learned how to swim again using her prosthetic tail. Winter even starred as herself in two movies about her.

Aiding a Gator

An alligator named Mr. Stubbs lost his tail. Without his tail, he could drown. So doctors at the Phoenix Herpetological Society created a prosthetic tail for Mr. Stubbs. The doctors studied how big his tail should be so he could swim. The tail took a while to make, but it greatly helped the alligator.

After Mr. Stubbs received a bionic tail, he could walk straighter and swim.

Deep Dive

Bionic Bird

An African penguin, Pierre, lost a lot of his feathers. Penguins molt once a year. That means they lose all their feathers before growing them back. But Pierre's feathers didn't grow back. Penguins' feathers are waterproof, which keeps them warm during and after they swim. Pierre was cold without his feathers.

The California Academy of Sciences created a wet suit for Pierre. It kept Pierre warm. Eventually Pierre's feathers grew back so he no longer needed the wet suit.

Pierre wears his wet suit made of neoprene, a rubberlike material.

Bionic devices are helping animals on land, in the air, and underwater. From beaks to flippers, bionic devices are making the future brighter for a lot of animals.

BIONICS CONTINUES TO SOLVE PROBLEMS IN THE ANIMAL WORLD.

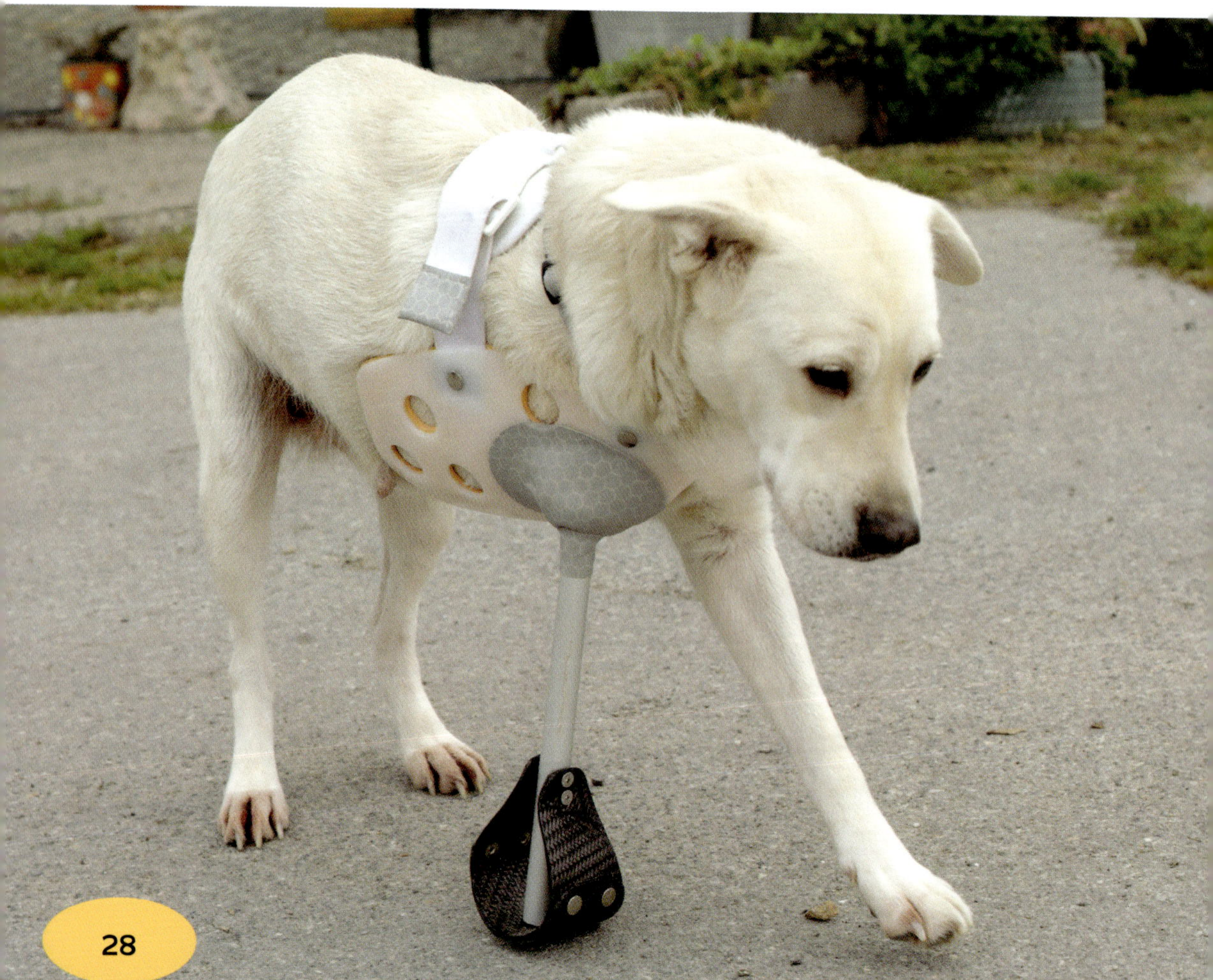

Save the Day

Bionic limbs don't work for every animal. Before giving an animal a bionic limb, veterinarians want to make sure the new limb will help the animal.

They can see if the animal is having a hard time because of an injury or missing limb. Then they will see how much of the limb is left. If a land animal lost part of a leg but still has the knee, a bionic limb might work. What are some other factors that might help decide if an animal should get a prosthesis?

Glossary

amputate: to remove a body part

engineer: a person who designs and builds machines and structures

limb: a leg or arm

material: a substance from which something is made or can be made

orthotics: a branch of medicine that deals with designing and fitting medical support devices

predator: an animal that kills and eats other animals to live

pressure: the weight or force that is made when something presses or pushes against something else

prosthesis: an artificial device that replaces a missing or injured part of the body

rehabilitation: the process of bringing someone or something back to a healthy condition after an illness or injury

technology: the use of science in industry, engineering, etc., to invent useful things or to solve problems

Learn More

Britannica Kids: Bionics
https://kids.britannica.com/students/article/bionics/273221

Idzikowski, Lisa. *Pet Tech.* Minneapolis: Lerner Publications, 2024.

Kiddle: Winter (Dolphin) Facts for Kids
https://kids.kiddle.co/Winter_(dolphin)

The Kid Should See This: Bionic Kangaroo
https://thekidshouldseethis.com/post/82207643065

Rathburn, Betsy. *Bionic Pets*. Minneapolis: Bellwether Media, 2021.

Swanson, Jennifer. *Beastly Bionics: Rad Robots, Brilliant Biomimicry, and Incredible Inventions Inspired by Nature*. Washington, DC: National Geographic, 2020.

Index

Photo Acknowledgments

Image credits: REUTERS/Alamy, p. 5; M Y Agency/Shutterstock, p. 6; REUTERS/Kevin Lamarque/Alamy, pp. 7, 15; DiveDesign, p. 8; AP Photo/Alexandr Kryazhev/Sputnik, p. 9; Claudia Rocchini, p. 11; AP Photo/The News Tribune/Lui Kit Wong, pp. 12, 13; Mees Kuiper/Shutterstock, p. 14; AP Photo/Young Kwak, p. 17; Kent Gilbert/Xinhua/Alamy, p. 18; REUTERS/Juan Carlos Ulate/Alamy, p. 19; Medical University of Vienna, pp. 20, 21; AP Photo/Eric Gay, p. 23; Auckland University of Technology Biodesign Lab, p. 24; AP Photo/Chris O'Meara, p. 25; Phoenix Herpetological Sanctuary, p. 26; AP Photo/Eric Risberg, p. 27; Dubravka Petric/PIXSELL/Alamy, p. 28.

Front cover: DiveDesign.